THE ESSENTIALS OF SPIRITUALITY

A Jewish Theological Argument On the Implicit Worth
And Eminent Potential of Every Human Being

by Felix Adler

Originally published 1908

The Essentials of Spirituality

The first essential is an awakening, a sense of the absence of spirituality, the realized need of giving to our lives a new and higher quality; first there must be the hunger before there can be the satisfaction.

Similar effects are often produced by widely differing processes. In the psychical world that quality which we call spirituality may be associated with and evoked by Theism, or the belief in a Divine Father; by Pantheism, as in the case of Spinoza, whose face at the very first glance impresses you with its spiritual cast; or even by the Buddhist belief in Nirvana. It may also be attained by following the precepts and striving after the ideals of Ethical Culture. For spirituality is not indissolubly associated with any one type of religion or philosophy; it is a quality of soul manifesting itself in a variety of activities and beliefs.

Before we proceed further, however, we must hazard a definition of the word. In the region of mental activity which is called the spiritual life vagueness is apt to prevail, the outlines of thought are apt to be blurred, the feelings aroused are apt to be indistinct and transitory. The word 'spiritual' becomes a synonym of muddy thought and misty emotionalism. If there were another word in the language to take its place, it would be well to use it. But there is not. We must use the word 'spiritual,' despite its associations and its abuse. We shall endeavor, however, to attach a distinct and definite meaning to the word. Mere definition, however, is too abstract and nakedly intellectual. Perhaps a description of some types of character, combined with definition, will be the better way.

Savonarola is surely one of the commanding figures in history. His fiery earnestness, his passion for righteousness, the boldness with which he censured the corruptions of the Roman Court, the personal qualities by which he—a foreigner and a mere monk—made himself for a short period the lawgiver, the prophet, and virtually the dictator of Florence—that Florence which was at the time the very gemmary of the Renaissance—his sudden fall and tragic death; all combine to attract toward him our admiration, pity, and love, and to leave upon our minds the impression of his extraordinary moral genius. And yet, though a spiritual side was not wanting in Savonarola, we should not quote him as an outstanding exemplar of spirituality. The spiritual life is unperturbed and serene. His nature was too passionate, he was too vehement in his philippics, too deeply engrossed in the attainment of immediate results, too stormy a soul to deserve the name of spiritual.

Again, our own Washington is one of the commanding figures in history. He achieved the great task which he set himself; he secured the political independence of America. He became the master builder of a nation; he laid securely the foundations on which succeeding generations have built. He was calm, too, with rare exceptions; an expert in self-control. But there was mingled with his calmness a certain coldness. He was lofty and pure, but we should hardly go to him for instruction in the interior secrets of the spiritual life. His achievements were in another field. His claim to our gratitude rests on other grounds. The spiritual life is calm, but serenely calm; irradiated by a fervor and a depth of feeling that were to some extent lacking in our first president. Lincoln, perhaps, came nearer to possessing them.

Again, we have such types of men as John Howard, the prison reformer, and George Peabody, who devoted his great fortune to bettering the housing of the poor and to multiplying and improving schools. These men—especially the latter—were practical and sane, and were prompted in their endeavors by an active and tender benevolence. Yet we should scarcely think of them as conspicuous examples of the spiritual quality in human life and conduct.

Benevolence, be it never so tender and practical, does not reach the high mark of spirituality. Spirituality is more than benevolence in the ordinary sense of the term. The spiritual man is benevolent to a signal degree, but his benevolence is of a peculiar kind. It is characterized by a certain serene fervor which we may almost call saintliness.

But perhaps some one may object that a standard by which personalities like Savonarola, Washington, Howard and Peabody fall short is probably set too high, and that in any case the erection of such a standard cannot be very helpful to the common run of human beings. Where these heroic natures fall short, can you and I hope to attain? To such an objection the reply is that we cannot be too fastidious or exacting in respect to our standard, however poor our performance may be. Nothing less than a kind of divine completeness should ever content us. Furthermore, there have been some men who approached nearer to the spiritual ideal than the patriots and the philanthropists just mentioned—some few men among the Greeks, the Hindus, and the Hebrews. And for the guidance of conduct, these more excellent spirits avail us more than the examples of a Savonarola, a Washington or a Howard. To be a prophet or the lawgiver of a nation is not within your province and mine. For such a task hardly one among millions has the opportunity or the gifts. To be liberators of their country has been accorded in all the ages thus far covered by human history to so small a number of men that one might count them on the fingers of a single hand. Even to be philanthropists on a large scale is the restricted privilege of a very few. But to lead the spiritual life is possible to you and me if we choose to do so. The best is within the reach of all, or it would not be the best. Every one is permitted to share life's highest good.

The spiritual life, then, may be described by its characteristic marks of serenity, a certain inwardness, a measure of saintliness.

By the latter we are not to understand merely the aspiration after virtue or after a lofty ideal, still pursued and still eluding, but to a certain extent the embodiment of this ideal in the life—virtue become a normal experience like the inhalation and exhalation of breath! Moreover, the spiritually-minded seem always to be possessed of a great secret. This air of interior knowledge, of the perception of that which is hidden from the uninitiated, is a common mark of all refinement, aesthetic as well as moral. In studying the face of Leonardo da Vinci's 'Mona Lisa,' for instance, one will find that it is this interior insight that explains the so-called "cryptic smile." In the case of aesthetic refinement, the secret discloses itself as at bottom delicacy, the delicacy which prevents intrusion on the personality of others; which abhors a prying curiosity; which finds subtle ways of conveying esteem and delicate modes of rendering service. But the secret of moral refinement is of a far higher order, transcending aesthetic refinement by as much as goodness is superior to mere charm. The secret in this case consists in the insight vouchsafed to the spiritually-minded of the true end of human existence.

Constituted as we are, there exist for us lower and higher ends.

This distinction is fundamental for ethics. Food is necessary; without it we cannot live. But the getting of food—however necessary—is a lower end. Knowledge is a necessary end, and a higher one. The practical moral ends, such as the reformation of prisons, the improvement of the dwellings of the poor, are yet higher ends. But above all these is the highest end, that of moral completeness, of perfection, not in one particular but in every particular. Spirituality consists in always keeping in view this supreme end. The spiritually-minded person is one who regards whatever he undertakes from the point of view of its hindering or furthering his attainment of the supreme end. If a river had a consciousness like the human consciousness, we might imagine that it hears the murmur of the distant sea from the very moment when it leaves its source, and that the murmur grows clearer and clearer as the river flows on its way, welcoming every tributary it receives as adding to the volume which it will contribute to the sea, rejoicing at every turn and bend in its long course that brings it nearer to its goal. Such is the consciousness of a spiritually-minded human being. Or to take a simile from human experience. There are times when we go abroad to travel just for change of scenery and the refreshment which change brings with it. When we go in this mood we are likely to be intent on wayside pleasures, and at every stage of the journey, at every town where we halt, we shall suffer ourselves to be engrossed in the points of interest which that temporary abiding-place has to offer us, careless of what may await us farther on. But there are other times when we go abroad on serious business. Some congress of scientists or fellow-workers is to meet in which we are to take our part; or there is a conflict being waged in which we are to bear our share of wounds or death, as in the case of the Japanese, who are now setting out from their homes toward the battlefields of Manchuria; or there is some loved one at a distance who needs us, calls us, expects us. Then the stations on the way are unable to captivate our attention; we are impatient to pass them by; we welcome each one as we approach it as bringing us one step nearer to the desired goal.

Some such analogy will help us understand the inner state of a spiritually-minded person. He thinks always of the ultimate end.

In whatever he does or omits to do he asks himself, Will it advance me or divert me from the ultimate goal? Since spirituality consists in keeping in mind the ultimate goal, it follows, in accordance with what was said in the beginning, that there must be various types of spirituality, corresponding to the various ways in which the ultimate goal is conceived. For those to whom the final end of human life is union with God, the Divine Father, the thought of this Divine Father gives color and complexion to their spiritual life.

They think of Him when they lie down at night and when they rise up in the morning; his praise is ever on their lips; the desire to win his approbation is with them in all their undertakings. To those who regard the attainment of Nirvana as the supreme end, like the Buddhists, the thought of Nirvana is a perpetual admonition. To those who view the supreme end of life as moral perfection, the thought of that perfection is the constant inner companion. The moral man, commonly so-called; the man who is honest, pays his debts, performs his duties to his family; the man who works for specific objects, such as political reform; this man, worthy of all respect though he be, is still intent on the stages of his journey.

The spiritual man, as we must now define him from the point of view of Ethical Culture, is the man who always thinks of the ultimate goal of his journey, i. e., a moral character complete in every particular, and who is influenced by that thought at all times and in all things. Spirituality, in this conception of it, is nothing but morality raised to its highest power.

And now, let us ask what are some of the conditions on which the attainment of such a life depends. The prime condition is to acquire the habit of ever and anon detaching one's self from one's accustomed interests and pursuits, becoming, as it were, a spectator of one's self and one's doings, escaping from the sweeping current and standing on the shore. For this purpose it is advisable to consecrate certain times, preferably a certain time each day, to self-recollection; to dedicate an hour—or a half-hour, if no more can be spared—to seeing one's life in all its relations; that is, as the poet has put it, to seeing life "steadily and seeing it whole." The sane view is to see things in their relation to other things; the non-sane view is to see them isolated, in such a way that they exercise a kind of hypnotic spell over us. And it makes no difference what a man's habitual interests may be, whether they be sordid or lofty, he needs ever and anon to get away from them. In reality, nothing wherewith a man occupies himself need be sordid.

The spiritual attitude does not consist in turning one's back on things mundane and fixing one's gaze on some supernal blaze of glory, but rather in seeing things mundane in their relation to things ultimate, perfect.

The eating of bread is surely a sufficiently commonplace operation. Yet Jesus brake bread with his disciples in such way that that simple act has become the symbol of sublimely spiritual relations, the centre of the most august rite of the Christian Church. In like manner the act of sitting down to an ordinary meal with the members of our family may, if seen in its relations, be for us a spiritual consecration. The common meal may become for us the type of the common life we share, the common love we bear.

On the other hand, seemingly much more lofty pursuits may have a narrowing and deadening effect on us if we do not see them in their ultimate relations, and so divest them of reference to life's highest end. For instance, the pursuit of science may have this effect, if the sole object of the scientist be to perform some astonishing piece of work for the purpose of attracting attention or to secure a well-salaried position, or even if he be so wedded to his specialty as to fail to be sensitive to the relations of it to the body of truth in general. And the same holds good of the narrow-minded reformer, of whom Emerson has said that his virtue so painfully resembles vice; the man who puts a moral idol in the place of the moral ideal, who erects into the object toward which all his enthusiasm goes some particular reform, such as the single tax, or socialism, or public parks, or a model school; the man, in short, who strives for a good instead of striving for goodness. Whatever our pursuits may be, we should often mentally detach ourselves from them, and, standing aloof as impartial spectators, consider the direction in which they are taking us.

This counsel is frequently urged on grounds of health, since the wear and tear of too intense absorption in any pursuit is apt to wreck the nervous system. I urge it on the ground of mental sanity, since a man cannot maintain his mental poise if he follows the object of his devotion singly, without seeing it in relation to other objects. And I urge it also on the ground of spirituality, for a salient characteristic of spirituality is calmness, and without the mental repose which comes of detachment we cannot import calmness into our lives. There are some persons, notably among those engaged in philanthropic activities, who glory in being completely engrossed in their tasks, and who hug a secret sense of martyrdom, when late at night, perhaps worn out in mind and body, they throw themselves upon their couch to snatch a few hours of insufficient sleep. Great occasions, of course, do occur when every thought of self should be effaced in service; but as a rule, complete absorption in philanthropic activity is as little sane and as little moral as complete absorption in the race for gain. The tired and worn-out worker cannot do justice to others, nor can he do justice to that inner self whose demands are not satisfied even by philanthropic activity. If, then, self-recollection is essential, let us make daily provision for it. Some interest we should have—even worldly prudence counsels this much—as far remote as possible from our leading interest; and beyond that, some book belonging to the world's great spiritual literature on which we may daily feed.

The Bible used to be in the old days all-sufficient for this purpose, and it is still, in part at least, an admirable aid to those who know how to use it. But there are other books, such as the legacy of the great Stoics, the writings of our latter-day prophets, the essays of Arnold and Carlyle and Emerson, the wisdom of Goethe. These noble works, even if they do not wholly satisfy us, serve to set our thoughts in motion about high concerns, and give to the mind a spiritual direction.

A second condition of the spiritual life has been expressed in the precept, reiterated in many religions, by many experts in things relating to the life of the soul: "Live as if this hour were thy last."

You will recall, as I pronounce these words, the memento mori of the Ancients, their custom of exhibiting a skeleton at the feast, in order to remind the banqueters of the fate that awaited them.

You will remember the other-worldliness of Christian monks and ascetics who decried this pleasant earth as a vale of tears, and endeavored to fix the attention of their followers upon the pale joys of the Christian heaven, and you will wonder, perhaps, that I should be harking back to these conceptions of the past. I have, however, no such intention.

The prevailing attitude toward the thought of death is that of studied neglect. Men wish to face it as little as possible. We know, of course, what the fate is that awaits us. We know what are the terms of the compact. Now and again we are momentarily struck by the pathos of it all; for instance, when we walk through some crowded thoroughfare on a bright day and reflect that before many years this entire multitude will have disappeared. The rosy-cheeked girl who has just passed; the gay young fellow at her side, full of his hopes, confident of his achievements, acting and speaking as if the lease of eternity were his; that "grave and reverend seigneur," clad with dignity and authority—all will have gone, and others will have taken their places. Yet, as a rule, we are not much affected by such reflections. When one of our friends has met with a painless death we are apt to solace ourselves with the hope that perhaps we shall be as lucky as he; at all events, we know that when our time comes we must take our turn. Even those who look forward with apprehension to the last moment, and who when it approaches, cling desperately to life, are prudent enough to hold their peace. There is a general understanding that those who go shall not mar the composure of those who stay, and that public decorum shall not be disturbed by outcries.

This is the baldly secular view of the matter, and this view, though based on low considerations, in some respects is sound enough.

And yet I reiterate the opinion that to live as if this hour were our last—in other words, to frankly face the i.e. of death—is most conducive to the spiritual life. It is for the sake of the reflex action upon life that the practice of coming to a right understanding with death is so valuable. Take the case of a man who calls on his physician, and there unexpectedly discovers that he is afflicted with a fatal malady, and is told that he may have only a few months longer to live. This visit to the physician has changed the whole complexion of life for him. What will be the effect upon him? If he be a sane, strong, morally high-bred man, the effect will be ennobling; it will certainly not darken the face of nature for him.

Matthew Arnold wished that when he died he might be placed at the open window, that he might see the sun shining on the landscape, and catch at evening the gleam of the rising star.

Everything that is beautiful in the world will still be beautiful; he will thankfully accept the last draught of the joy which nature has poured into his goblet. Everything that is really uplifting in human life will have a more exquisite and tender message for him. The gayety of children will thrill him as never before, interpreted as a sign of the invincible buoyancy of the human race, of that race which will go on battling its way after he has ceased to live. If he be a man of large business connections, he will still, and more than ever, be interested in planning how what he has begun may be safely continued. If he be the father of a family, he will provide with a wise solicitude, as far as possible, for every contingency. He will dispose of matters now, as if he could see what will happen after his departure. On the other hand, all that is vain or frivolous, every vile pleasure, gambling, cruelty, harsh language to wife or child, trickery in business, social snobbishness, all the base traits that disfigure human conduct, he will now recoil from with horror, as being incongruous with the solemn realization of his condition.

The frank facing of death, therefore, has the effect of sifting out the true values of life from the false, the things that are worth while from the things that are not worth while, the things that are related to the highest end from those related to the lower partial ends. The precept, "Live as if this hour were thy last," is enjoined as a touchstone; not for the purpose of dampening the healthy relish of life, but as a means of enhancing the relish for real living, the kind of living that is devoted to things really worth while. As such a test it is invaluable. The question, "Should I care to be surprised by death in what I am doing now?"—put it to the dissipated young man in his cups, put it to the respectable rogue—nay, put it to each one of us, and it will often bring the blush of shame to our cheeks. When, therefore, I commend the thought of death, I think of death not as a grim, grisly skeleton, a King of Terrors, but rather as a mighty angel, holding with averted face a wondrous lamp. By that lamp—hold it still nearer, O

Death—I would read the scripture of my life, and what I read in that searching light, that would I take to heart.

Finally, there is a third condition of the spiritual life which I would mention, and which comes nearer to the heart of the matter than anything that has yet been said. Learn to look upon any pains and injuries which you may have to endure as you would upon the same pains and injuries endured by someone else. If sick and suffering, remember what you would say to someone else who is sick and suffering, remember how you would admonish him that he is not the first or the only one that has been in like case, how you would expect of him fortitude in bearing pain as an evidence of human dignity. Exhort yourself in like manner; expect the same fortitude of yourself. If any one has done you a wrong, remember what you would adduce in palliation of the offence if another were in the same situation; remember how you would suggest that perhaps the one injured had given some provocation to the wrongdoer, how you would perhaps have quoted the saying: "Tout comprendre est tout pardonner"—"to understand is to pardon," how you would in any case have condemned vindictive resentment. In the moral world each one counts for one and not more than one. The judgment that you pass on others, pass on yourself, and the fact that you are able to do so, that you have the power to rise above your subjective self and take the public universal point of view with respect to yourself, will give you a wonderful sense of enfranchisement and poise and spiritual dignity.

And, on the other hand (and this is but the obverse of the same rule), look upon everyone else as being from the moral point of view just as important as you are; nay, realize that every human being is but another self, a part of the same spiritual being that is in you, a complement of yourself, a part of your essential being.

Realize the unity that subsists between you and your fellow-men, and then your life will be spiritual indeed. For the highest end with which we must be ever in touch, toward which we must be ever looking, is to make actual that unity between ourselves and others of which our moral nature is the prophecy. The realization of that unity is the goal toward which humanity tends.

Spirituality depends upon our tutoring ourselves to regard the welfare of others—moral as well as external—as much our concern as our own. What this practically means the following illustration will indicate. A certain bank official, a man of excellent education and of high social standing, committed a crime. He allowed himself in a moment of lamentable weakness to use certain trust funds which had been committed to him to cover losses which he had sustained. He intended to replace what he had taken, of course, but he could not do so, for he became more and more deeply involved. One night as he was alone in his office it became plain to him that the day of reckoning could no longer be put off. He was at the end of his resources. The morrow would bring exposure and ruin. Then the temptation seized him to make away with himself.

He had a charming wife and two lovely daughters. He was the revered head of the household; in the eyes of his family the paragon of honor. He was universally esteemed by his friends, who knew not his temptation and his fall. On that night in the lonely office he could not bear to think of meeting the future, of being exposed as a criminal in the eyes of his friends, of bringing upon his family the infamy and the agony of his disgrace. Should a man in his situation be permitted to commit suicide? If we were at his elbow should we allow him to do so? This question was submitted to one of my Ethics classes. The students at first impulsively decided in the affirmative, for they argued, as many do, that right conduct consists in bestowing happiness on others, and wrong conduct in inflicting suffering on others; and now that the man had committed the crime, they maintained he could at least relieve those whom he loved of his presence by taking himself out of their way. True, someone said, the exposure was inevitable in any case, and the shock of discovery could not be averted; but we were forced to concede that from the point of view of suffering, the pain involved in the sudden shock could not be compared to the long-drawn-out anguish which would result if he continued to live.

For presently he would forfeit his liberty; he would sit as a prisoner in the dock. His wife and daughters, loyal to their duties even toward an unworthy husband and father, would be found at his side. They would hear the whispers, they would see the significant nods, they would endure all the shame. Later on, when the trial was at an end, the prisoner would stand up to hear the verdict.

They would still be near him. Still later there would be the pilgrimage to the prison on the Hudson. They would see their beloved husband and father in striped garb among the scum and refuse of society, and these weary journeys would be repeated during long years until his term was over and he returned a broken and outcast man to what was once a home. Could not this lamentable issue at least be forestalled? But then there came a new light into our discussion. One of the students suggested that he must face the consequences of his wrongdoing, and that one of the consequences is the very suffering which he inflicts upon the innocent. He must see that day by day. That would be a part of his expiation, the purifying fire that may consume the dross of his nature. And, on the other hand, it would be right for the innocent to bear, not the guilt, but the consequences of the guilt of the wrongdoer whom they have loved, whom they still love. For this is the holy law: that the other whom we love shall be taken into our self as a part of our very self, that in his joy we shall rejoice as if his joy were ours, that in his achievements we shall triumph, that in his humiliations we shall be humbled, and that we shall work out his redemption by traveling with him the hard road that leads out of the dark depths upward again to the levels of peace and reconciliation.

The spiritual life depends on self-recollection and detachment from the rush of life; it depends on facing frankly the thought of death; it is signalized, especially, by the identification of self with others, even of the guiltless with the guilty. Spirituality is sometimes spoken of as if it were a kind of moral luxury, a work of supererogation, a token of fastidiousness and over-refinement. It is nothing of the sort. Spirituality is simply morality carried to its farthest bounds; it is not an airy bauble of the fancy, it is of "the tough fibre of the human heart."

II. THE SPIRITUAL ATTITUDE TOWARD ONE'S NEIGHBOR.

Sunday, Nov. 27, 1904.

Those whom we call our neighbors, our fellow-men, may stand to us in a threefold relation. Some possess gifts far greater than our own, and in point of development are our superiors; some are on the same level; and some are much inferior to us. The spiritual attitude toward our neighbor—though always governed by the same principle, expresses itself in different ways, according as our neighbor is related to us in one or another of these three ways.

I recently read a biography of Matthew Arnold, the author of which constantly speaks of himself as Arnold's disciple. It is not often nowadays that we hear men proclaim themselves disciples and glory in their discipleship. At the present day the tendency is for every one to assert an equality with others; and most persons would resent the imputation of subordination implied in such a word as disciple. And yet the writer in question is a self-respecting man, he is thoroughly alive to his dignity, and he has keen and unsparing words for certain of the faults of the master whom he reveres. He is not blind, he is not wax in the hands of the master, he does not look upon him with undiscerning admiration, and yet he takes toward him the reverent attitude—what I should call the spiritual attitude—for he recognizes that this master of his is a casket in which nature has deposited a treasure of extraordinary value, that he possesses a genius much superior to that of others.

The loyal disciple is concerned that this genius should appear in its full potency and in undiminished radiance. To this end is the upward look, the appreciation and reverence, and to this end also the misgiving and the remonstrance when the great man deviates from the course which he ought to follow. The same attitude of loyalty we sometimes find among the disciples of great artists, and the followers of great religious teachers. Loyalty is a virtue which is somewhat underrated at the present day. Loyalty is not debasing, not unworthy of a self-respecting man; it is but another name for the spiritual attitude toward those who have a superior genius, to whose height we are lifted by our appreciation of them.

Furthermore, in our spiritual relation toward those who occupy about the same plane of development with ourselves, the same principle of sympathy with the best possible attainment should be the rule. To rejoice in the failure of others, to accentuate in our thinking and in our conversation the faults of others, to triumph at their expense, is the utterly unspiritual attitude. To desire that others may manifest the excellence that is latent in them— be it like to or different from our own, to desire that they shall have credit for every excellence they possess, and to sedulously aid them in developing such excellence as they can attain to, that is the spiritual attitude.

I have spoken of superiors and equals, of our attitude toward those who are more developed than we are, and toward those who are about equally developed; but my address to-day will be mainly occupied with our duty toward those who are or seem to be wholly undeveloped. The fundamental principle of Ethics is that every human being possesses indefeasible worth. It is comparatively easy to apply the principle of anticipating our neighbor's latent talents to the highly gifted, to the great authors, scientists, statesmen, artists, and even to the moderately gifted, for their worth is, in part, already manifested in their lives. But it is not so easy to apply or justify the principle in the case of the obscure masses, whose lives are uneventful, unilluminated by talent, charm, or conspicuous service, and who, as individuals at least, it might appear, could well be spared without impairing the progress of the human race. And yet this doctrine of the worth of all is the cornerstone of our democracy. Upon it rests the principle of the equal rights of even the humblest before the law, the equal right of all to participate in the government. It is also the cornerstone of all private morality; for unless we accept it, we cannot take the spiritual attitude toward those who are undeveloped.

The doctrine, then, that every man possesses indefeasible worth is the basis of public morality, and at the same time the moral principle by which our private relations to our fellow-men are regulated. What does it mean to ascribe indefeasible worth to every man? It means, for instance, that human beings may not be hunted and killed in sport as hunters kill birds or other game; that human beings may not be devoured for food as they have been by cannibals or sometimes by men in starvation camps when hard pressed by hunger; that human beings may not be forced to work without pay, or in any way treated as mere tools or instruments for the satisfaction of the desires of others. This, and more to the same purpose, is implied in the ascription of indefeasible worth to every man. Moreover, on the same principle, it follows that it is morally wrong to deprive another of the property which he needs for his livelihood or for the expression of his personality, and to blast the reputation of another—thereby destroying what may be called his social existence. And it also follows that a society is morally most imperfect, the conditions of which are such that many lives are indirectly sacrificed because of the lack of sufficient food, and that many persons are deprived of their property through cunning and fraud. The life of animals we do take, and whatever secret compunction we may have in the matter, the most confirmed vegetarian will not regard himself in the light of a cannibal when he partakes of animal food. The liberty of animals we do abridge without scruple; we harness horses to our carriages, regardless of what may be their inclinations, and we do not regard ourselves as slaveholders when we thus use them. Why is there this enormous distinction between animals and men? Are the Hottentots so greatly elevated above the animal level; are the lowest classes of negroes so much superior in intelligence to animals? Have the black race and the brown race any claim to be treated as the equals of the white? Among white men themselves is there not a similar difference between inferiors and superiors? Such questions naturally suggest themselves; and they have been asked at all times. It seems obvious that value should be ascribed to those who possess genius or even talent, or at least average intelligence; but why should value be ascribed to every human being just because he wears the human form?

The positive belief in human worth on which is based the belief in human equality, so far as it has rooted itself in the world at all, we owe to religion, and more particularly to the Hebrew and Christian religions. The Hebrew Bible says: "In the image of God did He create man"—it is this God-likeness that to the Hebrew mind attests the worth of man. As some of the great masters on completing a painting have placed a miniature portrait of themselves by way of signature below their work, so the great World-Artist when He had created the human soul stamped it with the likeness of Himself to attest its divine origin. And the greatest of the Hebrew thinkers conceived of this dignity as belonging to all human beings alike, irrespective of race or creed. In practice, however, the i.e. of equal human worth was more or less limited to the Chosen People. At least, to keep within the bounds of the artistic simile, the members of the Hebrew people were regarded as first-proof copies, and other men as somewhat dim and less perfect duplicates.

In the Christian religion a new i.e. was introduced. The belief in the worth of man was founded on the doctrine of redemption. The sacrifice of atonement had been offered up for the benefit of all persons who chose to avail themselves of it. Christ had come to save the Gentile as well as the Jew, the bond as well as the free, men, women and children of every race, living under every sky, of every color of skin and degree of intelligence. The sacred respect which we owe to every human being is due from this point of view to the circumstance that every human being is a possible beneficiary of the Atonement. For him too—as the theological phrase is—Christ died upon the cross. But in Christianity too we find that the i.e. of brotherhood, of equal worth, universal as it is in theory, in practice came to be considerably restricted. It did not really extend to all human beings as such; it did not extend to those who refused to be the beneficiaries of the act of atonement.

In reality, it applied only to Christians or to those who were not averse to receiving the Christian faith. The theological formulation of the fundamental i.e. which we are discussing, therefore, is beset by two difficulties: it is limited in application, and it is based on theological conceptions. As soon as these theological conceptions are relinquished, the doctrine of equality is in danger of being abandoned.

In 1776, the founders of the American Republic undertook to supply a new and a secular foundation for this doctrine. In the Declaration of Independence, Jefferson wrote: "We hold these truths to be self-evident, that all men are created free and equal."

In other words, he put forth the astonishing proposition that human equality is self-evident. Many of us would incline to the opinion that the opposite is self-evident, that the inequalities which subsist between men are so palpable that we cannot overlook them. If, however, we inquire what led Jefferson to this statement, we shall find that, at the time when the Declaration of Independence was written, there existed a basis of fact that gave color to his assumption. The population of the United Colonies was small—only about three millions—and on the whole homogeneous. The great majority of the people were agriculturists, pursuing the same occupations and on the whole exhibiting the same traits. They were all, or almost all, of vigorous stock, capable of self-government, jealous of their rights, independent in spirit. At that particular time, the points of similarity and equality among the members of the American Colonies far outweighed the points of dissimilarity. It was, then, to a certain extent on facts of experience, and not entirely on the hypothesis of the eighteenth century philosophy, that Jefferson's famous proclamation rested.

Since Jefferson's day the facts have markedly changed. We have passed beyond the agricultural stage, and have entered the stage of industrial development. The occupations of our citizens have become greatly diversified. Large bodies of foreign immigrants have come to us. If we survey the conditions of American life at present, we are strongly impressed with the differences that exist between the various strata of our population: differences in mental ability, differences in vital energy, differences in the point of culture attained, differences in capacity to rise. As a consequence, the Declaration of Independence is treated by many as an obsolete document, and its assertions as mere bombast and rhetoric; unjustly so, because the truth which it attempts to convey is valid, though the form in which the truth is expressed and the grounds on which it is put are no longer adequate.

We have arrived, then, at this pass: the theological foundation for the doctrine of human equality has failed or is failing us; the facts to which the Declaration of Independence appealed have altered. Are we, then, to give up the belief in human equality—that priceless postulate of the moral law, the basis alike of democracy and of private morality? At times it seems to us that the world is almost ready to do so. Nietzsche in Germany puts it forth as a philosophic principle that humanity exists not for the democratic purpose of securing the highest development of all, but for the aristocratic purpose of producing a race of supermen, an elite of strong, forceful, "leonine" beings. And in his doctrine that the many exist as a kind of pedestal for the grandeur of the few, he finds support the world over. Men are but too ready in this age, when the energies of the strong have been unfettered and moral restraints have become weakened, to put Nietzsche's doctrine into practice too. From the Congo we hear appalling accounts of the cruelty of civilized men in their dealings with the uncivilized.

Rubber and ivory, it appears, must be obtained in large quantities to secure a handsome profit on investments that have been made in those regions. Railroads must be built to make the supply of rubber and of ivory accessible. In consequence, a system of forced labor, of virtual slavery, has been imposed on the miserable natives in order to make the building of these railroads possible. Human life has not been spared, for human life in the Congo is as dust in the balance when weighed against the profits from rubber. Punitive expeditions have been organized (in other words, wholesale slaughter has been resorted to), in order to coerce the reluctant natives to bring in their supplies more punctually. The wives and daughters of the natives have been seized, brutally chained, and detained as hostages in order to influence their husbands and fathers to a more ready obedience. The story of the Congo reads like an incredible nightmare; the civilized world is aghast at the partial revelations of it which have been published. From Armenia we hear similar stories of ruthless contempt for human life and merciless outrage. With Kishineff and Siberia in mind, we need not comment on the conditions that exist in Russia. In the United States, the heartrending circumstances that accompany negro lynchings, the conditions in the sweated industries, and the widespread evil of child labor show us clearly enough how little the doctrine of the intrinsic and indefeasible worth of man has as yet become the property of even the most advanced nations. In the face of all these odds on the other side, in the face of these confederate forces working the world over for the abasement of man, how urgent is the appeal to rescue and fortify the doctrine, to make it effectual, first in our own conduct and then in that of others! And on what tenable foundations can we rest it, that it may become operative?

First, as to its meaning. It does not mean equality of gifts, or equality of mental energy, or equality in any of the traits that lead to successful careers. It means equality in the sense that each is the vehicle of some talent, however small, the bearer of some gift, however seemingly inconsiderable, which in the sum total of humanity's development is needed; that each one in his place and with his gift, however insignificant in appearance, is in fact indispensable.

And what is the reason for ascribing such worth to human beings?

The sole reason is, that the moral law enjoins us to do so. Before ever we have discovered whether a man has worth in him or not, the moral law enjoins us to ascribe it to him, to treat him as if he had it, to see in him the light of the possibilities which he has never made good and which he never wholly will make good: and thus, and thus only, shall we bring to light, in part at least, the precious things in his nature, the existence of which we can only divine. The moral law is wholly misunderstood if it be founded on the actual worth or value of men, for none of us has great worth or value.

The moral law is a law for the eliciting of possibilities. Briefly put, it enjoins that we shall invest others with a garment of light, that we shall ascribe worth to others and to ourselves, in order that they and we may become worthy. This is the spiritual basis of the doctrine of equality; this is the spiritual conception which should regulate our attitude toward our neighbors.

And yet if there were no evidence at all to support our faith in human goodness, our faith, however vigorous at first, would soon decline, and hope and courage might utterly desert us. If men on nearer acquaintance turned out to be, as some pessimists have represented them to be, hard egotists, ingrates, slanderers, backbiters, envious, incapable of generous admirations, sodden in sensuality, knaves devoid of scruple; if experience indeed bore out this sweeping impeachment, if especially the so-called masses of mankind were hopelessly delivered over to the sway of brutal instincts, of superstition and folly; the faith of which I speak might justly be termed mere fatuousness, and the rule of acting on the assumption that men are better than they appear would turn out a blind delusion. But the striking fact is, that as soon as we act on the principle of looking for the latent good in others, we are rewarded by finding far more than we had any reason to expect.

Take as an instance the masses of the poor and ignorant, upon whom we are so apt to pass sweeping judgments, as Carlyle did when he said that the population of England was forty millions—mostly fools. The experience of those who have had to do with popular education does not corroborate this rash condemnation.

There is hardly a child in our public schools that is not found to possess mental power of some sort, if only we possess the right method of calling it out. The new education is new and significant just because it has succeeded in devising methods for gaining access to the latent mental power, and thus reaching what had been supposed to be non-existent. Every so-called educational campaign in the field of politics brings out the same truth. The capacity for hard thinking and sound judgment which resides in the working class is surprising to us, only because in our preposterous pride we had supposed them to be baked of different clay than we are. In the matter of artistic endowment, too, what wonderful discoveries do we constantly make among poor children, even among children that come from the lowest dregs of society! What fine fancy, what prompt response to the appeal of the beautiful, in spite of all the debasing inheritance!

But it is, in the last analysis, the moral qualities upon which our respect for human nature rests, and in this respect how often are we astonished, yes and abashed, when we observe the extent to which the moral virtues express themselves in the life of those who, in point of so-called culture, are infinitely our inferiors! What power of self-sacrifice is displayed by these poor people, whom sometimes in our wicked moods we are disposed to despise; what readiness to share the last crust with those who are, I will not say hungry, but hungrier! Who of us would take into his own house, his own bedchamber, a dying consumptive, a mere acquaintance, in order that the last days of the sufferer might be soothed by friendly nursing? Who of us would make provision in our will to share our grave with a worthy stranger, in order to avert from him the dreaded fate of being buried in the Potter's

Field? Which of our young men would be willing to refuse the proffered opportunity of an education in one of the foremost colleges in the land, in order to stay with the old folks at home and work at a menial occupation for their support? Who of us would give up the joys of youth to devote his whole life to the care of a bed-ridden, half-demented parent? Yet all of these things and many others like them I have known to be done by people who live in the tenement houses of this great city. It sometimes seems as if the angelic aspect of human nature displayed itself by preference in the house of poverty, as if those who possessed no other treasure, no other jewels with which to adorn themselves, were compensated for their penury in other ways by these priceless gems of the most unselfish virtue. Such conduct, of course, is not universal. There are abundant instances of the opposite. But the truth remains that it is the worth which those who seem to lead the least desirable lives display toward others that assures us of their own worth.

This, too, is the lesson of the oft-quoted and oft-misunderstood parable of the Good Samaritan, upon which here, for the moment, I should like to dwell.

The Jewish State in the time of Jesus was substantially an ecclesiastical aristocracy. The highest rank was occupied by the priests and their assessors, the Levites; after them, sometimes disputing the first place, came the doctors learned in the sacred law; below them the commonalty; and still lower in the social scale were the people of Samaria, who accepted the current Jewish religion only in part, and who were regarded by the blue-blood ecclesiastical aristocrats with contempt, indeed almost as outcasts.

This fact it is necessary to remember in order to understand the parable. The designation Good Samaritan has become so associated with the i.e. of mercifulness, that

I doubt not there are many persons who have the impression that Samaritans in the ancient Hebrew days were people specially noted for their benevolent disposition. Nothing of the kind, of course, is true. The Samaritans were a despised lower stratum of the population of Palestine. Read the parable in this light, and you will perceive that the moral of it is not as commonly stated— every one who has need of me is my neighbor; but that there is a far deeper meaning in it.

There came to Jesus one day a man versed in the sacred law, and asked him what he must do to inherit eternal life. And Jesus replied: The substance of right conduct is plain enough. Why do you ask as if it were a thing very recondite and difficult? Love thy God and thy neighbor. But the doctor of the sacred law, wishing to justify himself (wishing to show that the way of the upright life is not so plain, that it may be difficult to decide whom one should regard as one's equal, to whom one should ascribe worth), asked: Who is my neighbor? And Jesus replied in the words of the well-known parable concerning a certain man who had fallen among thieves, and these stripped him of his raiment and left him for dead on the public road that runs between Jerusalem and Jericho.

Presently a member of the high aristocracy, a priest, passed by, but paid no attention to the sufferer; then another, a Levite, came that way, looked at the man who was lying there helpless, and turned and went on his journey. Then there came one of those low-caste despised Samaritans; and he acted like a tender human brother, bound up the man's wounds, poured oil and wine into them, etc.

And Jesus said: Which one of these three showed himself to be a neighbor to the man that had fallen among thieves? In which of the social classes did there appear to be the truest understanding of the conduct which moral duty requires of us toward our fellow-men—in the upper classes or in the lowest? And the answer evidently is—in the lowest. The point of the parable is that the Samaritan himself, whom priest and Levite and doctor of the law refused to regard as a neighbor, was worthy to be treated as a neighbor, because he understood, as they did not, how to treat others as neighbors.

The lesson of the parable is a twofold one: not only that the wounded man lying untended on the road was a neighbor because of his need, but more especially that the Samaritan was a neighbor because he responded to the need, and set an example of truly human behavior to those who had doubted whether, because of his extreme social degradation, he was himself to be regarded as human.

The moral qualities in men, then, constitute their most universal title to respect, and these qualities we find in all social grades and among all races and nationalities. We find them among the Chinese, as their devoted family life, the honesty of their merchants, and the ethics of Confucius indicate. We find them among the negroes, not only in the case of exceptional persons like Booker Washington or Dubois or Atkinson, but also in the undistinguished life of many an obscure man and woman, whom to know more intimately is to learn to respect as a neighbor and a moral equal. What we need to build up our faith in human goodness is the clairvoyance that discerns the hidden treasures of character in others. And one other quality is indispensable for the moral appreciation of our neighbors, namely, the quality of humility. Strange as it may seem, the less we plume ourselves on our own goodness, the more we shall be ready to believe in the goodness of other people; the more we realize the infinite nature of the moral ideal and our own distance from it, the more we shall esteem as of relatively small importance the distance that separates us from others, the slight extent to which we may morally surpass them. The more we are aware of our own frequent and serious shortcomings, the more, when we perceive the moral delinquencies of others, shall we recognize in their nature the same recuperative agency which we believe to be in ourselves, namely, the power of divine regeneration that can make all things new. If we regard ourselves as morally little and yet as never lost, we shall regard no one else as lost, however morally little he may seem to be.

Respect, then, for the indefeasible worth of every human being must be based not on theological systems which are fast decaying, nor on the fancied self-evidence of Jefferson's Declaration, but solely on the moral law which commands us to ascribe such worth to others whether we perceive it or not, nay, to create it in others by ascribing it to them.

Such is the spiritual attitude toward our fellow-men. And though our confidence may not always be demonstrably justified by the result, though we not always succeed in uplifting others, yet by pursuing this line of conduct we ourselves at all events shall be uplifted, our own life will be touched to finer issues.

III. THE SPIRITUAL ATTITUDE TOWARD OPPRESSORS.

Sunday, Dec. 4, 1904.

The problem of our spiritual attitude toward positive badness, social and individual wrongdoing, cruelty and oppression, is far more difficult of solution than the problem of our attitude toward worth really existent but concealed. The thorny question, how we are to deal with wicked persons, whether we are to observe the spiritual attitude toward them, and in what that attitude consists, requires the most sincere and straightforward treatment.

Should we cultivate an attitude of indifference in such cases? A ruffian cruelly beats his horse, the poor beast that has rendered him faithful service for many a day, but is feeble now and sinks beneath its load. With curses and the sharp persuasion of the lash, the merciless driver seeks to force the animal to efforts of which it is plainly incapable. Can we stand by and witness such a scene in philosophic calm? Shall we say that the wretch is the product of circumstances, and cannot be expected to act otherwise than he does? Shall we liken evildoers generally, as at present is customary in certain quarters, to the sick? Shall we say that such men are the outcome of their heredity, their education, their environment? I have known of a husband who in a state of intoxication brutally struck and injured his wife, while she was holding in her arms a babe not eight days old. Shall we say that that man was morally sick, that he could not help becoming intoxicated, and therefore was not responsible for the havoc he wrought when the demon of drink had gained possession of him? Shall we say of the syndicate of traders who hunt the natives on the Congo like rabbits, massacre and mutilate them, that they are sick? A bad deed done with intention argues badness in the doer. We impute to the man the act and its consequences. We cannot separate the sin from the sinner, and merely condemn sin in the abstract. There is no such thing as sin in the abstract. Sin is sin only when it is incorporated in the will of a human individual. We condemn the sinner because he has wedded himself to the sin. If this were not the case, we might as well close our courts of justice. We hold men accountable, then, for their misdeeds, whatever speculative philosophy may urge to the contrary. How could we revere virtue if we did not stigmatize its opposite; how could we believe in human worth if we did not condemn unworth where it appears?

But the ordinary judgment stops short right here. It recognizes the particular badness of a particular act, and desires that the agent be made to suffer for it. It says, this act is the expression of an evil disposition, and it identifies the whole man with the particular act of which he was guilty. The spiritual attitude is characterized by discriminating between the particular act and the whole of the man's nature. It recognizes that there is an evil strand; but it also sees or divines the good that exists along with the evil, even in the most seemingly hopeless cases. It trusts to the good, and builds upon it with a view to making it paramount over evil. Upon the basis of this spiritual attitude, what should be our mode of dealing with the bad? There are a number of steps to be taken in order, and much depends on our following the right order.

The first step is to arrest the course of evil, to prevent its channel from being deepened, its area from being enlarged. Pluck the whip from the hand of the ruffian who is lashing his beast; stay the arm that is uplifted to strike the cowardly murderous blow. Much has been said of the need of considering the good of society, of protecting the community at large from the depredationsof the violent and fraudulent; and of subjecting the latter to exemplary punishment, in order to deter others from following their example.

But the welfare of society and the welfare of the criminal are always identical. Nothing should be done to the worst criminal, not a hair of his head should be touched merely for the sake of securing the public good, if the thing done be not also for his private good. And on the other hand, nothing can be done to the criminal which is for his own lasting good that will not also profoundly react for the good of society, assuring its security, and deterring others from a like career of crime. The very first claim which the criminal has upon the services of his fellow-men is that they stop him in his headlong course of wickedness. Arrest, whether by the agents of the law or in some other way, is the first step. The most spiritual concern for a degraded and demoralized fellow-being does not exclude the sharp intervention implied in arrest, for the spiritual attitude is not mawkish or incompatible with the infliction of pain.

This, I think, will be readily granted. But the second step, a step far more important than the arrest of the evildoer in order to arrest the evildoing, is more likely to be contested and misunderstood.

The second step consists in fixing the mark of shame upon the offender and publicly humiliating him by means of the solemn sentence of the judge. It may be asked, What human being is fit to exercise this awful office of acting as judge of another? Remember the words of Shakespeare in King Lear: "… .See how yond justice rails upon yond simple thief. Hark in thine ear: change places; and … . which is the justice, which the thief?" Or recall what the Puritan preacher said when he saw from his window a culprit being led to the gallows: "There, but for the grace of God, go I." In other words, had I been born as this man was, had I been played upon by the influences to which he was subject, had I been tempted as he was, how dare I say that I should not have fallen as he did? Had it not been for some grace extended to me through no desert of mine, I might be traveling the road on which he travels now.

Furthermore, can we say that the sentence of the judge is proportioned to the heinousness of the deed? Is the murderer who in a fit of uncontrolled passion has taken a human life—it may have been his first and only crime—necessarily more depraved than the thief; or is the thief in jail who has indeed broken the law, necessarily more depraved than numbers of others who have dexterously circumvented the law, violating the spirit though keeping within the letter of it? Is even the abject creature who strikes his wife more abandoned than a man of the type of Grandcourt in Daniel Deronda, whose insults are dealt with a marble politeness, and who crushes his wife's sensibilities, not with a vulgar blow but with the cold and calculating cruelty of a cynic?

When it comes to passing moral judgments and fixing blame, and especially to measuring the degree of another's guilt, who of us is good enough, who of us is pure enough, who of us is himself free enough from wrong to exercise so terrible an office? Is not Lear right, after all: "… .change places; and… .which is the justice, which is the thief?"

It may be said in reply to these objections: First, that the judge does not speak in his private capacity, but that he delivers the judgment of mankind on the doer and the deed, serving as the mouthpiece of the moral law, so far as it is incorporated in the human law. We should select the highest characters available for so exalted a duty, but freedom from even great human infirmity we cannot expect to find. Again, it is not the judge's business to fix the degree of moral guilt; that not even the best and wisest of men can do. The inscrutable fact of the degree of moral guilt eludes all human insight. Only omniscience could decide who is more guilty relatively to opportunities, advantages, circumstances; who has made the braver effort to escape wrongdoing; whether the admired preacher, or the culprit on his way to the gallows; whether the President in the White House or the wretch behind the bars. The office of the judge is to pronounce that crime has been committed, irrespective of the subtle question of the degree of guilt. Murder has been done, property has been stolen, the sin and the sinner wedded together. The office of the judge is to declare the fact of that infelicitous union, and to pronounce the penalty according to the law. And this, in particular. The object of the punishment which the law pronounces is not vindictive chastisement of the culprit. The object of punishment is purely reformatory. Only it must not be forgotten that there can be no reformation without penitence, and no penitence without self-abasement. And this consists in confessing one's self guilty, admitting that the guilt has become a part of one's being, and humbling one's pride to the ground. The public sentence pronounced by the judge, the shame which he fixes upon the culprit, has, then, for its object to pave the way toward reformation, to break down the defenses which the sophistry of wickedness sets up, to compel the man to see himself as others see him, to force him to realize to the full the evil of his present state. Not to blast him utterly, not to exclude him forever from the kindly society of men, but to lead him into the way along which—if he travel it—he may eventually return, though perhaps only after many years, to human fellowship. If the verdict is pronounced in any other spirit, it is false and inhuman. The methods to be employed to bring about reformation must often be severe and painful, and one of these methods is shock, shock sharp and sudden enough to loosen the incrustations of evil habit, and to shake a wicked nature down to its foundations. The purpose of the trial of a criminal in a court of justice, and of the verdict in which the trial culminates, is to supply such a shock, a searching and terrible experience, yet salutary and indispensable in order that better things may ensue.

From what has been said, it follows that the death penalty as a punishment even for the worst crimes is morally untenable; for either the culprit is really irredeemable, that is to say, he is an irresponsible moral idiot, in which case an asylum for the insane is the proper place for him; or he is not irredeemable, in which case the chance of reformation should not be taken from him by cutting off his life. The death penalty is the last lingering vestige of the Lex Talionis, of the law which attempts to equalize the penalty with the crime, a conception of justice which in all other respects we have happily outgrown. It does not necessarily follow that the immediate abolition of capital punishment is expedient. It is not expedient in fact, because of the condition of our prisons, and because of the abuses to which the pardoning power of the State is subjected; because security is lacking that the worst offenders, before ever they can be reclaimed, may not be returned unrepentant into the bosom of society, to prey upon it anew with impunity. But, then, we must not defend the death penalty as such, but rather deplore and do our utmost to change our political conditions, which make it still unwise to abolish a form of punishment so barbarous and so repugnant to the moral sense.

The step which follows the arrest and condemnation of the evildoer is isolation, with a view to the formation of new habits. A change of heart is the necessary pre-requisite of any permanent change in conduct; but the change of heart, and the resolution to turn over a new leaf to which it gives birth, must be gradually and slowly worked out into a corresponding practice. The old body of sin cannot be stripped off in a moment; the old encumbrance of bad habits cannot be sloughed off like a serpent's coil. The new spirit must incorporate itself slowly in new habits; and to this end the delinquent must be aided in his efforts by a more or less prolonged absence from the scene of his former temptations.

He must be placed in an entirely new and suitable environment, and encouraging pressure must be exerted upon him to acquire new habits of order, diligent application to work, obedience, self-control. It is upon this i.e. that the moral propriety of imprisonment and of prison discipline is based, whether the actual treatment of prisoners be in accord with it or not.

And so we may pass on at once to the last and chief element in the process of the reclamation of the evildoer, namely, forgiveness.

An angel's tongue, the wisdom and insight of the loftiest of the sages, would be required to describe all the wealth of meaning contained in the sublime spiritual process which we designate by the word pardon. It is a process which affects equally both parties to the act, the one who forgives and the one who is forgiven. It exalts both, transfigures both, indeed establishes a new tie of wonderful tenderness and sublimity between them. The person who forgives is a benefactor.

Is it a little thing, when a man is sunk in the slough of poverty, denuded of all the decencies of life, harassed day and night by grinding cares, knows not whither to turn to find shelter and food, for some fellow human being, moved by pure human kindness, or let us rather say moved by respect for the worth which he sees in his perishing fellow-man, to come to the aid of the latter, to lift him out of his distress, to place him on sun-lit levels, to put him on his feet and give him a new chance, to open for him a new career in which effort may meet with its reward? Such an act of human helpfulness is not a little thing; the man who does it is rightly esteemed a great benefactor. Or is it a little thing to save the imperiled sick, to bring back from the brink of the grave a precious life, already despaired of? This, too, surely is not a little thing, and the good physician who accomplishes such a miracle is rightly esteemed a benefactor to whom lifelong gratitude is due.

But there is a yet greater thing, a benefit, by the side of which even these—great as they are—appear almost insignificant. To take a man who is sinking in the moral slough and has no courage left to rise out of it; to give him back his lost self-esteem, that jewel without which health and wealth are of little avail; to put him in a position once more to look his fellow-men straight in the eye; to place him morally on the sun-lit levels; to put him morally on his feet—this assuredly is the supreme benefit, and the man who accomplishes this for another is the supreme benefactor. And a note of exquisite moral beauty is added if the benefactor be the same person whom the guilty man had injured. This is what is meant by forgiveness. This is why forgiveness is so divine a thing.

This is the reason why, when an act of genuine forgiveness occurs, "the music of the spheres" seems to become audible in our nether world. And this is also the reason why we often see such a strange kind of tie springing up between a person who has been chastised and the one who has chastised him in the right spirit and then forgiven him—a tie into which there enters shame for the wrong done, gratitude for the unmerited good received, and a reverence akin to idolatry toward the one upon whose faith in him the sinner rebuilt his faith in himself.

There should be some organ of the State to exercise this office of forgiveness toward criminals, this pardoning power in the finer sense of the term. The prison warden, if he be a man of the right stamp, sometimes exercises it. The Society for the Befriending of Released Prisoners has here an appropriate function open to it; also the employer who after due inquiry has the courage to dismiss suspicion and to give work to the released prisoner.

The methods and principles which I have described in the case of the criminal are used for illustration, not that I am interested today in discussing the special problem of the criminal, but because principles can best be exemplified in extreme cases. The same methods, the same maxims should control punishment in general; our dealings, for instance, with the misdeeds of which our own children are guilty. Here, too, there should be by no means unvarying gentleness and pleading, but when need arises the sharp check, that evil may be instantaneously stopped. Here, too, there should be the temporary disgrace, the clear presentation of the magnitude of the fault, if it have magnitude, the humiliation that calls forth penitence and good resolutions. Here, too, there should be sedulous care, to work out the better habits. And all these steps should be taken with a view to ultimate reconciliation, forgiveness, and the holier bond between parent and child.

But now can we take one step further? Can we dispose our minds and our hearts in the same fashion toward oppressors? I have in mind, for instance, the hard proprietors of houses who pitilessly wring the last penny from their tenants; the cruel taskmasters who drive the workers, sometimes only children not yet full-grown, twelve and fifteen hours a day; the unscrupulous exploiters on a large scale, who raise the price of the people's food, and in their eagerness for fabulous gain conspire by every corrupt means to crush their less crafty or less shameless competitors. As we hate wrong, must we not hate them? Shall we assail greed and exploitation merely in the abstract? What effect will that have?

Which one of the oppressors will not hypocritically assent to such abstract denunciation? If we seek to produce a change, must we not proceed to more specific allegations and point the finger of scorn at the offenders, saying as the Prophet Nathan said to King David: "Thou art the man"? Is it not necessary to arouse the popular anger against the oppressors and to encourage hatred against the hateful?

Clearly the case is not the same as that of the criminal in the dock.

He stands there dishonored; the evil he has done has been brought home to him; he is covered with the garment of shame. But those others are invested—despite the evil they have done and are still doing—with every outward symbol of success; they triumph defiantly over the better moral sense of the community; they inhabit, as it were, impregnable citadels; they have harvested unholy gains which no one seems strong enough to take from them; and the influence they wield in consequence of their power to benefit or harm is immense. Is it a wonder, then, that such oppressors are branded as monsters, and that the hoarse note of some of the Hebrew psalms is sometimes to be heard re-echoing in the cry of the social radicals of our time—Let vengeance be visited upon the wicked; let the oppressors be destroyed from the face of the earth!

But the logical and inevitable conclusion of the thought I have developed to-day is, that we are bound to recognize the indefeasible worth latent even in the cruel exploiter and the merciless expropriator. I have already sufficiently indicated that the spiritual view is consistent with severe and stringent treatment.

Checks there should be by the heavy hand of legislation laid upon the arrogant evildoers. They should be stopped if possible in mid-career. The oppressed, also, should oppose those who oppress them. No one is worth his salt who is not willing to defend his rights against those who would trample on them. So far from ruling out conflict, I regard conflict as a weapon of progress—an ethical weapon, if it be waged with the right intentions.

Furthermore, when speaking of oppression, I have in mind not merely the cupidity of the few as it operates mercilessly upon the many, but also the banded arrogance of the many as it sometimes displaysitself in contempt for the rights of the few. From whichever side oppression proceeds, there should be resistance to it; the check imposed by resistance is one of the means of educating to new habits those who find themselves checked.

Individuals, and social classes, too, as history proves, learn to respect the rights which they find in practice they cannot traverse.

First come the limits set to the aggression, and then the opening of the eyes to perceive the justice of the limitation. But conflict is an ethical weapon only if it is wielded like the knife in the surgeon's hands. The knife wounds and hurts; the method is apparently cruel; but the purpose is benevolent. So should the battle of social reform be animated by concern not only for the oppressed, but also for the oppressor. And such a motive does not exceed the capacity of human nature, but, on the contrary, is the only motive which will permanently satisfy human nature. Certain of the Socialists have made it their deliberate policy for years to stir up hatred between the poor and the rich, on the ground that hatred alone can overcome the lethargy of the masses and arouse in them the intensity of feeling necessary for conflict. On the contrary, hatred engenders hatred on the opposite side, action provokes reaction.

As the individual can be uplifted in his life only by accepting the spiritual motive, by trying to act always so as to recognize in others and to make manifest the indefeasible worth of the human soul, so the social classes can be uplifted only by acting on the same spiritual motive.

Despite the efforts of a hundred years, the real progress that has been achieved in ameliorating the relations between the social classes at the present day is slight, and sometimes one is impelled to doubt whether there has been any progress at all. The egotism of one side is met by the egotism of the other side. But appeals to mass egotism will no more elevate mankind, than appeals to individual egotism. Appeals to sympathy also will not permanently help. Only the highest motive of all can furnish the power needed to accomplish the miracle of social transformation; only that conflict which is waged for the purpose not of striking down the oppressor and rescuing his victim, but for the rescue of both the victim and the oppressor, will attain its end.

The oppressor may be regarded as a man who has consented so to degrade himself as to become for the time being a heartless automaton, ruthlessly working for gain, a being like one of those terrible ogres of the popular mythology who feed on human flesh.

But he is not a mere automaton or ogre. There is a better side to his nature, as we often discover, to our amazement, when we learn about the facts of his private life. These private virtues do not indeed condone his social sins—far from it—but they indicate that there exists a better side. If that side could be made victorious, if conditions could be shaped so as to starve out the worse nature and bring to the fore the better nature in the oppressor as well as in the oppressed, the problem would be advanced toward a solution.

There is a story told of two brothers, sons of the same father, who grew up in the same home and were deeply attached to each other.

It happened that the older wandered away and fell into the power of an evil magician, who changed him into a ravening wolf. The younger mourned his loss, and treasured in his heart the image of the brother as he had been in the days before the wicked spell fell upon him. Impelled by his longing, he at last went out into the world to find his brother, and if possible to redeem him. One day as he passed through a lonely forest, a hungry wolf set upon him.

The horrid, brutal face was near to his, the hot breath breathed upon him, and the fierce eyes flamed into his own. But by the might of his love, the younger brother was able to detect beneath the wolfish disguise the faint outlines of the brother whom he had long ago lost, and by the strength of his gaze, which saw only the brother and refused to see the wolf, he was able to give shape and substance to that faint outline. The outer frame of brutishness gradually melted away, and the human brother was restored to his senses and to his home. This is a parable of the spiritual attitude toward oppressors, toward those who oppress the people in public, as well as toward those who oppress us in our private lives.

We must liberate them from the brutal frame in which they are inclosed; we must give them back their human shape!

IV. THE TWO SOULS IN THE HUMAN BREAST

Sunday, Dec. 11, 1904.

Painful and revolting associations are called up by the phrase—"leading the double life." To the aversion provoked by the evil itself, is added in such cases the disgust excited by the hypocrisy with which it is cloaked. He who leads a double life offends not only by the wrong he does, but by borrowing the plumes of virtue.

He lives a perpetual lie; he is "a whited sepulchre, clean on the outside, full of filth and corruption within." The Beecher trial at the time so profoundly agitated the whole country, because the accusations brought forward associated the name of one of the most prominent characters of the nation, a man of brilliant talent and meritorious service, with secret impurity. The more meritorious such a man's services, the more damning the charges if they be established. Nor do we admit in such cases the sophistical argument, that the interests of public morality require the facts to be hushed up in order to avoid a scandal. Nothing is so imperative where guilt really exists as that it be confessed and expiated. The public conscience requires the truth. Let the sinner make a clean breast of it; let the atmosphere be cleared by an act of public humiliation. No injury to the cause of public morality is so great as the lurking suspicion that men who stand forth as exponents of morality are themselves corrupt. Lurking suspicion, distrust of all the moral values, is worse than recognition of human weakness, however deplorable.

There are other examples of the double life, with which all who have knowledge of the world's ways are familiar. That of the merchant, for instance, who, though he has long been virtually a bankrupt, conceals his position behind a screen of opulence, emulating the sumptuous expenditure of the rich, living a life of glittering show; tortured inwardly by the fear of exposure, yet not courageous enough to be honest; sinking deeper himself and, what is worse, dragging others down with him. A young man at college sometimes leads a double life, his letters home being filled with accounts of his legitimate employments, while at the same time he is leading the life of the prodigal, the spendthrift, the dissipated sot.

The dual life has been depicted in powerful colors by poets and writers of fiction; as, for instance, by Hawthorne in his "Scarlet Letter," by Robert Louis Stevenson in his "Doctor Jekyll and Mr.

Hyde." I suppose if there be such a thing as hell on earth, the double life is another name for it. Yet I know of no writer of fiction whose plummet has sounded the depths of this hell. In Stevenson's story one gets the impression of a too mechanical separation between the two sides. The man is at one moment the benevolent doctor, and at another the malignant fiend. The device of the drug is introduced to explain the transition; but the transformation is too sudden, too abrupt. Jekyll and Hyde dwell side by side in the same body, and the relations between them have not been wrought out with sufficient subtlety. It is rather a broad moral parable than a subtle study of man's dual nature.

The initial point I desire to make is, that in certain cases the inner torture and anguish of the dual life can only be ended by publishing the secret, so long and jealously hidden. Just as the criminal must stand judgment in a court of law, so must the double-minded man stand judgment in the court of public opinion. It is not possible to determine by a hard and fast line, when such exposure is obligatory; but in general it may be said that it is required in those cases where publicity is necessary to set things right and to repair the wrong that has been done to others.

There are, however, cases in which others are not affected, or only indirectly so; in which the evil relates to the personal life and its consequences are private to the man himself. The situation is such as is described by Goethe, when he speaks of the two souls dwelling within the human breast; the soul itself in its own sphere being divided against itself. The man is conscious of rectitude in one part of his conduct, of magnanimous impulses, of high and noble aspirations. He feels himself allied on one side to what is best and purest, and at the same time is aware of another side which in his saner moments fills him with loathing, and poisons for him life's cup of satisfaction. It is of this class of cases that I propose to speak. And here the terrible fact stares us in the face, that if the dual life be interpreted in this sense, there is hardly a man who is not leading it. Even the best of men have been aware of an abhorrent side of their nature. What else can St. Paul mean when he speaks of the continual warfare between the two laws—"the law of the flesh that is in his members, and the law of God that is in his spirit"? What else do the confessions of St.

Augustine reveal but the continual oscillations of a finely poised nature between the two extremes? What else can we gather from certain passages in Tennyson's writings, but hints of a miserable and grievous struggle of the same sort? And what an intolerable burden to anyperson of integrity, to any one who would at least be honest, to think that he passes for better than he is, to think that if men only could see his heart as he sees it, they would pass him by with scorn instead of admiration! Yet as a rule, in such cases self-revelation is not only not demanded, but not even allowable.

The opening of the secret chambers of one's life to the public, confessions like those of Rousseau, are, if anything, indecent and nauseating. The case of a man in such situations is bad enough, but the remedy for it is perforce committed to his own hands. Let him put his hand to the plough and not turn back, let him grapple with the evil in his nature and subdue and transform it, let him accomplish his inner redemption, let him make himself what he ought to be—what others perhaps think he is. What aid can the spiritual view of life extend to him in this stupendous business?

The cardinal thought I have in mind, which I believe will provide an escape from such intolerable moral dilemmas, can best be set forth by contrasting it with its diametrical opposite. This opposite is contained in the Buddhistic doctrine of the Karma. The doctrine of Karma implies that we are what we are to-day, good or bad, or good and bad, in consequence of good or bad deeds which we performed in previous states of existence. Our present life, according to this view, is but a link added to the chain of the innumerable lives which we have left behind us. It is true, we do not remember those past existences; but all the same, they have left their indelible mark upon us. Our fortunes, too, in this present existence, are determined by our meritorious or unmeritorious behavior in the past. If, for example, a man acts as your enemy to-day, it is because in a previous state you wantonly injured him or some one like him. Bear your disappointments, then, and the harm you receive from others without complaint; you are but suffering the penalty you deserve. Not only our fortune but our character, as has been said, is thus predetermined; we are what we are, in virtue of what we have been. If a man is a mean miser, it is because in a previous existence he was already unduly covetous of wealth. 'Tis but the seed he sowed in the past, that blossoms out in the present. If a man commit murder, it is because he was already guilty of unchecked violence in previous lives. The beginnings which he made in the past culminate in the awful present.

This is indeed a plausible theory, and it would help
us to read some dark riddles if it were true, but there is not
the slightest reason for supposing that it is. If ever there
was a theory in the air, this is one. We not only have no
recollections of any past incarnations, but we have no
ground for inferring that there were any. I have mentioned
the theory merely in order to exhibit its opposite. And the
opposite is this: that a man is not responsible for the
attractive or repulsive qualities with which he is born; that
these are not to be accounted as his, in the sense that he is
accountable for them. The son of the dipsomaniac, for
instance, is not responsible for the morbid craving that stirs
in him. He begins life, so far as responsibility is concerned,
so far as merit or demerit is concerned, with a fresh start.
He is not responsible for the craving; he is responsible only
for assenting to it. True, the pull in his case is
incomparably stronger than in others; still he can resist. He
is responsible, not for the hideous thing itself, but for the
degree in which he yields to it. He is meritorious to the
extent of the effort he puts forth not to yield to it. The
reason why this point is often obscured is that from the first
awakening of consciousness, from the time when first we
have been capable of deliberate choice, we have more or
less often assented to these evil propulsions and have thus
made them our own. It has therefore become impossible to
separate clearly between that element in our acts which is
imposed upon us from without, and that deliberate element
in the act which is our own. Nevertheless, no fair-minded
person will dispute that there are qualities or
predispositions, for which—hideous as they may be—we
are no more responsible than we are for being born with an
unprepossessing face. Men are born with certain attractive
qualities and certain atrocious qualities, but moral
goodness and badness consists not in having these

predispositions, but rather in consenting to them and adopting them into our will.

Now this, it seems to me, throws an entirely new light upon the duality of our inner life. The fact that we discover that there is baseness within us from which we recoil as we should from a venomous snake, need not shake our throne of reason or overthrow our balance. These base things are not we; our true self does not reside in them, until, indeed, we unite with them by assenting to them. A man's natural propensities are motley, but his soul is white. One hears much nowadays of the "white man's burden." There is such a thing as the white soul's burden. These dipsomaniac cravings with which some men are handicapped, these explosive irascibilities with which some are accursed, these tendencies to impurity with which others are defiled—these are the white soul's burden. Some men are more heavily burdened than others. But it is not the nature of the burden that makes men good or bad; it is the way they bear it, or rather it is the extent to which they transform this initial nature of theirs into a better nature.

There is a distinction between the natural character and the moral character; the moral character results from the changes produced in the natural character, by the power of the moral will, or by the energy of the soul striving to imprint its nobler pattern on this difficult, oft intractable material.

But if we are not blameworthy for the repellant propensities, neither are we praiseworthy on account of the attractive and gracious qualities we may possess. The state of mind of one who is conscious of a divided inner life is torture. Nothing but an heroic treatment, nothing but a radical cure will free him from that torture; the cure is to realize that our seeming virtues are often not virtues at all. We must sacrifice our fancied virtues, if we would escape from the horrid sense of utter depravity that arises from our vices. A man puts to himself the question: How is it possible that at one moment I should be sympathetic and kind, should strive to compass the happiness of my fellow-beings, should take a generous interest in public causes, and try to act justly; and that at another moment I am so selfish and base? How can there be this oscillation from one pole to the other of human character? It is the contradiction that makes the tragedy. Am I, too, not "truly one but truly two"; am I, too, a Jekyll and a Hyde, both dwelling under the same skin? The answer is: You are neither the Hyde nor the Jekyll unless you elect to be. The true self is a principle in you superior to both these natural characters, a kind of oversoul, as Emerson puts it.

Sympathy and kindness lend themselves to the building up of a virtuous character, they are the psychological bases of virtue, but they must not be confounded with virtue itself. Taken by themselves, they represent merely a felicitous mixture of the elements of which we are compounded, no more praiseworthy than their opposites are blameworthy. Sympathy and kindness must be governed and regulated by principle, if they are to be rated as moral qualities. Left uncultivated, they often produce positively immoral results. Likewise, what is called justice is often no more than a hard adherence to rules, a love of order in our relations to others, which must be tempered and softened by the quality of mercy, before it can be accounted a moral virtue. Again, a willingness to advance the interests of a class or of a people is often no more than an enlarged egotism, with most of the defects of the narrower egotism, and must be regulated by a moral principle, if it is to attain to the dignity of a moral attribute. It is only by the conformity of our thoughts, our feelings, and our acts to principle, that morality is achieved. It is only by such means that the genial and attractive tendencies of our nature are converted into genuine virtues, and the way of escape from the double life is along the line of the moral transformation of our seeming virtues.

Mend your virtues, and your vices will take care of themselves.

But if the illusion is dispelled that the goodness or badness of an action as it appears to the eye is the measure of the virtuousness or viciousness of the agent; if the principle that governs the act and the effort put forth to conform to the principle be recognized as the true standard by which we are to judge, then two consequences will follow with respect to the conduct of life. The first is that the seemingly petty occasions of life are to be treated as grand occasions in so far as a moral principle is involved. For instance, a petty falsehood spoken for the purpose of securing business advantage or of avoiding business loss may seem to the average man a trivial affair; and it is so, so far as the results are concerned. And yet a morally high-bred man could no more condescend to such a falsehood than a man of cleanly habits would willingly steep himself in the mire. It is not the consequences, one way or the other, that matter. It is the eternal issue between the moral realities, truth and untruth, that is at stake. And in the light of this issue, in the light of the principle involved, petty as the circumstances may be, the occasion is not to be considered trivial.

The eternal forces that have been at war since mankind first existed are at war on this occasion also; he must cast in his lot on the side of the good.

Another instance of action seemingly trivial is that of simulating a personal interest in others, of pretending agreement in the foibles of others or of affecting a personal homage which one does not feel, in order to use others as instruments for the achievement of one's ends, whether those ends be selfish pecuniary advantage or political

preferment, or even financial aid and support for some
important philanthropic enterprise. As if philanthropy—
which is based on respect for the worth of man—did not
defeat its own ends, the moment it seeks to accomplish
them by methods which degrade both him who gives and
him who receives. The occasion is small, but the principle
involved as to the choice of means is great. Another
instance relates to the degree to which we may trench upon
the personality of others, or seek to enter into that part of
their life which they keep secret from us. We may suspect,
for instance, that a friend is oppressed by some secret
trouble, and we may believe that we could help him if only
he would consent to reveal himself; but the act of self-
revelation must come from his side, and the permission to
help him must first be granted. We may give him the
opportunity to declare himself, but we may not invade the
sanctuary of his silence. The principle involved is great; it
is that of respect for the precincts within which every soul
has the right to live its own life.

And there are other illustrations in abundance that
might be quoted. For instance, custom prescribes rules of
behavior in respect to many things which are really
indifferent; in regard to the cut of the clothes we wear, in
regard to the accepted form of salutation, in regard to the
language of polite speech, and much more of the same sort.
Now, the ethically-minded man is not a pedantic
micrologist who wastes his time on the minutiae of
conduct. But where custom relates to things not indifferent,
where a principle is involved, there is no detail of conduct
so minute as not to challenge the most vigorous protest, the
utmost assertion of independence. The ethically-minded
man is one who endeavors to shake off the yoke of custom,
wherever it interferes with the affirmation of the great
principles of life; who disdains to follow the multitude in
doing not only what is palpably wrong, but what is morally

unfine. He seeks to be a free man, an independent being, and to assert without acrimony or invidious criticism of others, yet firmly and unflinchingly, a strong and self-poised manhood. This, then, is one consequence that flows from our point of view: namely, that in the moral sphere the small occasions are to be treated as if they were grand occasions. As the poet puts it, "Rightly to be great is not to stir without great argument, but greatly to find quarrel in a straw when honor is at stake," or, as we should put it, greatly to find quarrel in the straws of life when principle is at stake.

And the second consequence is the obverse of this: To treat what seem to be great occasions because of their outward results, as if they were small. Is it a fortune that smiles upon you, that you can win by suppressing a moral scruple, by transgressing the eternal law? Put it aside as a thing not worth a second glance, if the price exacted be the loss of self-respect, if the bargain to which you must subscribe be the betrayal of principle. Is it life itself that is at stake; the dear life to which we cling so fondly? Yes, life is precious in its nobler uses; but life itself shall not be esteemed as great in the hour in which we must choose between it and fidelity to principle. And that it is really possible to take this high attitude the example of the world's great martyrs shows.

* * *

The leading thoughts I have endeavored to state in these addresses are the following: Spirituality is morality carried out to the finish.

It depends on always keeping the ultimate end of existence in view, and on not resting in the partial ends. Intervals set aside for self-recollection and the facing of the thought of death are useful aids. The ultimate end itself is to elicit worth in others, and, by so doing, in one's self. The indispensable condition of this attitude is to ascribe worth to every human being before even we observe it, to cast as it were a mantle of glory over him, to take toward every fellow human being the expectant attitude, to seek the worth in him until we find it. Even toward oppressors we should take the same attitude. Furthermore, our true self resides neither in our poorer nor in our better natural endowments, but in the will that suppresses the one and alone gives moral significance to the other.

Finally, we must testify to our respect for principle by treating the small occasions of life as great if they involve a moral issue, and the great prizes of life as small if they are offered at the price of moral integrity. These are thoughts which I have found helpful in my own experience; I submit them to you, in the hope that they may be of use to you also.

Made in the USA
Columbia, SC
10 May 2020